MINDSET RULES!
A FUN AND PRACTICAL GUIDE TO MASTERING YOUR ENERGY AND MINDSET

KATHERINE MACLANE

KPM PUBLISHING

To my family—Henry, Charlie, Teddy, and Jared—your love and support are the foundation of my strength and inspiration.

To my clients, whose journeys of transformation inspire me daily.

And to my dear friend Anna Brooke, whose belief in my gifts set me on this path.

May this book help all who read it discover their own inner light and true potential.

CONTENTS

Introduction	vii
1. The Basics of Energy	1
2. The Power of Mindset	6
3. Mirror, Mirror on the Wall	11
4. The Art of Affirmation: Power in the Pen	15
5. Visualization: Crafting Your Future with a Mind's Eye	18
6. Breathwork: Mastering the Art of Breathing	21
7. Meditation for Mindset	25
8. Evidence Lists: Celebrating Small Wins	30
9. Creating an Energy Field: Cultivating Your Personal Space	34
10. Intention Setting: Your Daily Blueprint for Success	39
11. Segmenting Your Day: Mastering Transitions with a Smile	42
12. Finding Your Inner Glow	47
13. Creating Your Personal Energy and Mindset Chart: Your Daily Roadmap to Awesome	52
14. Real-Life Applications: Transformational Stories	55

Conclusion: Embrace Your Journey	61
Appendix	65
Resources for Further Learning and Support	67
Chakras	73
Understanding the Chakras	75
Balancing the Chakras	79
Affirmations	81
Affirmations for Relationship Issues (Spouse/Significant Other)	83
Affirmations for Career and Job Issues	85
Affirmations for Parenting and Child Issues	87
Affirmations for Financial Issues	89
Affirmations for Love and Relationships	91
Affirmations for Weight Issues	93
Affirmations for Health Issues	95
Affirmations for Aligning with Your Highest Self	97
Affirmations for General Well-being and Positivity	99
Visualizations	101
Visualization for Relationship Issues (Spouse/Significant Other)	103
Visualization for Career and Job Issues	105
Visualization for Parenting and Child Issues	107
Visualization for Financial Issues	109
Visualization for Love and Relationships	111
Visualization for Weight Issues	113
Visualization for Health Issues	115
Visualization for Aligning with Your Highest Self	117
Visualization for General Well-being and Positivity	119
Glossary	123
Acknowledgments	127
About the Author	129

INTRODUCTION

Introduction: The Magic of Energy and Mindset

Welcome to a journey that promises to be as enlightening as it is entertaining! If you've ever found yourself stuck in a rut, feeling like life's punching bag, or simply curious about how to harness the mystical powers of your own mind and energy, you're in the right place. Grab a cozy blanket, a cup of your favorite beverage, and let's dive into the world of energy healing and mindset transformation.

What on Earth is Energy Healing?

You might be thinking, "Energy healing? Is that like recharging my phone?" Well, not exactly, but close! Imagine your body is like a smartphone. Sometimes it gets bogged down with too many apps (or thoughts) running in the background, drains the battery (your energy), and starts to slow down or glitch (feeling tired or unwell). Energy healing is like giving your body a much-needed reboot, clearing out the unnecessary junk, and restoring it to its optimal state.

Energy healing is an ancient practice, kind of like yoga's wise old grandparent, that works with the unseen forces that flow within and around us. These forces are often referred to as your "energy field" or "aura." By balancing this energy, you can achieve greater physical, emotional, and mental well-being. Think of it as turning on the "Do Not Disturb" mode for your mind and body, allowing you to function at your best.

Understanding Mindset: Your Inner Narrator

Now, let's talk about mindset. Imagine you have a tiny narrator inside your head. Sometimes this narrator is a wise old sage, but more often than not, it's a grumpy gremlin who loves to point out everything that could go wrong. This is where mindset work comes in. By shifting from a negative, gremlin-infested mindset to a positive, sage-like one, you can transform your entire experience of life.

A positive mindset isn't about ignoring the bad stuff (like pretending you don't have 97 unread emails). It's about acknowledging challenges and choosing to focus on possibilities and solutions instead of problems. It's like swapping your dark, stormy glasses for a pair of rose-tinted ones. You still see the world, but in a much more flattering light.

Why Energy and Mindset Are Your New BFFs

So why should you care about all this energy and mindset mumbo jumbo? Well, because it's the secret sauce to a happier, healthier life! When your energy is balanced and your mindset is positive, you become unstoppable. You start to attract good things like a magnet, stress rolls off you like water off a duck's back, and you find joy in the simplest of moments.

Think about it: have you ever met someone who just seems to radiate positivity and good vibes? They're not born lucky; they've simply mastered their energy and mindset. And guess what? You can too! This book is your step-by-step guide to unlocking these superpowers within you.

We Create Our Own Energy

Here's the kicker: **we create our own energy with our thoughts, feelings, and emotions.** Imagine your mind is a factory, and your thoughts are the workers. Positive thoughts produce high-quality, vibrant energy that fuels your life and helps you thrive. Negative thoughts? Well, they churn out the equivalent of toxic waste that drags you down and makes everything harder.

Your feelings and emotions act as the quality control managers in this factory. When you feel happy, grateful, and hopeful, you generate positive energy that radiates outwards and attracts more of the same. On the flip side, when you dwell on fear, anger, or sadness, you create a cloud of negative energy that can darken even the sunniest days.

The good news is, you have the power to manage this factory. By consciously choosing positive thoughts and nurturing uplifting emotions, you can transform your energy and, by extension, your life. This book will show you how to become the master of your energy factory, ensuring that you produce the highest quality energy possible.

Personal Story: My Journey to Balance

Let me share a little story. Once upon a time, I was a hot mess. Seriously, a chaotic whirlwind of stress, self-doubt, and exhaustion. My days were a blur of endless to-do lists, and my nights were spent wide awake, worrying about all the things I didn't do. Then, I discovered energy healing and mindset work. But it didn't happen overnight. This has been a 15-year journey, step by step, discovering and playing with new tools.

When I finally started to get the hang of it, my first thought was, "Okay, so which one do I pick to teach?" I thought I had to choose between Reiki, Life Coaching, or one of the other certifications I picked up along the way. Then it hit me – I can combine them all. I can help clear energy and transform mindsets at the same time! It was like finding the instruction manual to my own brain and soul – and so rewarding to be able to share it!

Through mirror work, affirmations, visualization, and other techniques you'll soon learn, I went from feeling like a deflated balloon to a radiant, high-flying kite. My energy soared, my outlook brightened, and life became not just bearable but truly enjoyable. And now, I'm here to share these magical tools with you.

What to Expect in This Book

This book is divided into three parts. First, we'll cover the foundations of energy and mindset work, giving you the background you need to understand why these practices are so powerful. Next, we'll dive into the specific tools and techniques I use with my clients. Each chapter will introduce a new practice, complete with homework assignments (don't worry, these are the fun kind) and personal stories to illustrate their impact. Finally, we'll help you put it all together to create your personalized energy and mindset chart.

So, if you're ready to transform your life, laugh a little, and maybe even have some fun along the way, let's get started. Your journey to mastering your energy and mindset begins now. Ready? Set? Glow!

CHAPTER 1
THE BASICS OF ENERGY

Welcome to the first step of your journey into the mystical (but very real) world of energy. If you're imagining sparkly auras and mystical chants, you're partially right, but there's so much more to it. So, let's get comfortable, put on our favorite pair of metaphorical yoga pants, and dive into the basics of energy.

What is Energy?

Imagine you're a superhero. Not the cape-wearing, building-leaping kind, but one who harnesses the power of invisible forces to feel amazing and live your best life. That's what understanding energy is all about.

Energy is the life force that flows through everything. Yes, everything. That cup of coffee you're holding? It's buzzing with energy. Your cranky neighbor? Also filled with energy (though it might need a bit of balancing). We're all made of it, and it's constantly moving and interacting with the world around us.

. . .

The Energy Field: Your Invisible Shield

Think of your energy field as a protective bubble. It's a bit like the force field you'd see in a sci-fi movie, but less about deflecting laser beams and more about maintaining your inner zen. This energy field, or aura, surrounds your body and can be affected by your thoughts, emotions, and the environment.

When your energy field is balanced, you feel like you can conquer the world. When it's out of whack, it's like having a phone with a dying battery – everything feels harder and more draining. The good news is, you can learn to balance and boost your energy field with a few simple practices.

How Energy Affects Our Lives

Ever walked into a room and immediately felt the tension, like everyone just found out that the coffee machine is broken? That's your energy sensing the vibes around you. Energy affects how we feel, how we interact with others, and even how successful we are in our endeavors.

When your energy is high and balanced, you're like a magnet for positive experiences. People are drawn to you, opportunities seem to pop up out of nowhere, and life feels good. Conversely, when your energy is low, everything feels like a struggle. It's like trying to swim through molasses.

Keeping Your Energy in Check

So, how do you keep your energy field sparkling and balanced? Here's a sneak peek into some practices we'll dive deeper into later:

- **Mindful Breathing**: Just a few minutes of focused breathing can do wonders for your energy. Think of it as plugging yourself into a charger.

- **Visualization**: Picture yourself surrounded by a glowing, protective bubble of light. It sounds a bit woo-woo, but it works!

- **Grounding**: This involves connecting with the earth, either literally (like walking barefoot in the grass) or figuratively (visualizing roots growing from your feet into the ground).

- **Energy Clearing**: There are various techniques, like smudging with sage or using crystals, that can help clear out negative energy and keep your field bright and shiny.

The Science Behind Energy and Vibrations

Understanding how energy and vibrations affect us can seem a bit mystical, but there's actually some fascinating science behind it. Let me tell you a story about how even plants respond to vibrations in surprising ways.

The Magic of Vibrations: How Music and Birdsong Help Plants Grow

In the 1970s, a curious researcher named Dorothy Retallack conducted some experiments at Colorado Woman's College (Retallack, 1973). She wanted to see how different types of music affected plant growth. And guess what? Plants exposed to classical music thrived, while those subjected to harsh rock music often withered. This wasn't just a quirky experiment; it showed how vibrations and energy can profoundly impact living beings.

And Dorothy wasn't alone in her findings. Researchers in South Korea discovered that playing classical music to rice plants helped them grow faster and stronger. The sound waves seemed to enhance the plants' ability to take in nutrients and perform photosynthesis more efficiently.

But it's not just music that has this magical effect. Have you ever noticed how birds chirp early in the morning? Turns out, those cheerful songs might be doing more than just signaling the start of the day. Studies suggest that the vibrations from birdsong can actually stimulate plant growth. It's like nature's very own wake-up call for the plant world, nudging them to start their day.

Just like those plants, we too respond to vibrations and energy. Through mirror work, affirmations, and visualization, we can tune into the positive frequencies that help us thrive. Imagine yourself as a plant basking in the harmonious melodies of classical music or the natural songs of morning birds, growing stronger and more vibrant each day. That's the magic of energy work – and it's available to you.

Story: The Tale of the Energized Plant

Let me share a fun story. I once had a plant that was, to put it mildly, on death's door. No amount of watering or sunlight seemed to help. Then, a friend suggested I try talking to it with positive energy. I felt silly, but I gave it a shot. I stood by the plant, visualized it surrounded by a vibrant light, and spoke to it like it was my best friend. Within a week, that plant perked up and started thriving! Was it the positive energy? Of course!

Practical Exercise: Sensing Your Energy

Ready to get hands-on? Here's a simple exercise to start sensing your own energy:

1. Find a Quiet Space: Sit comfortably and take a few deep breaths.

2. Rub Your Hands Together: Generate a bit of heat and then slowly pull them apart.

3. Feel the Tingling: As you move your hands closer together and then apart again, you might start to feel a tingling or a slight resistance. That's your energy!

Take a moment to play with this sensation. It's like discovering you have a hidden superpower.

Wrap-Up

Understanding energy is the first step to mastering it. Remember, you're not just a body moving through space; you're a vibrant, energetic being with the power to transform your life. In the next chapters, we'll explore more tools and techniques to help you harness this energy and create the life you've always dreamed of. So, stay tuned, stay curious, and keep that energy field glowing!

CHAPTER 2
THE POWER OF MINDSET

By now, you've dipped your toes into the mystical waters of energy. But we're not done yet. It's time to talk about the other half of the dynamic duo: mindset. If energy is the fuel for your journey, mindset is the map that guides you. Buckle up, because we're about to embark on a mental adventure!

Understanding Fixed vs. Growth Mindset

Imagine your mind is like a garden. In a fixed mindset, your garden is full of rocks and weeds, with little room for growth. You believe your abilities and intelligence are set in stone, like those stubborn rocks. On the other hand, a growth mindset is like a fertile, well-tended garden where anything can flourish. You see challenges as opportunities to grow, and you believe you can cultivate new skills and abilities over time.

Fixed Mindset: The Garden of Doom

Let's get real for a moment. We've all had times when our inner narrator sounds like a grumpy old gremlin. "You're not smart enough," it grumbles. "Why even bother trying?" This is the fixed mindset at work. It thrives on self-doubt and fear of failure, turning every challenge into an insurmountable obstacle. It's like trying to grow roses in a rock garden – not happening!

Growth Mindset: The Garden of Possibilities

Now, picture this: a garden where the soil is rich, the sun is shining, and your plants (aka your skills and abilities) are thriving. This is the growth mindset. It's the belief that you can change, learn, and grow through effort and perseverance. Challenges become stepping stones, failures are just compost for future success, and your potential is limitless.

Shifting from Fixed to Growth Mindset

So, how do you uproot those pesky weeds of a fixed mindset and cultivate a lush garden of growth? Here are some practical tips:

1. Embrace Challenges: Instead of avoiding challenges, see them as opportunities to learn. It's like going to the mental gym – no pain, no gain!

2. Learn from Criticism: Constructive criticism is like fertilizer for your garden. It might smell a bit at first, but it helps you grow stronger.

3. Celebrate Effort, Not Just Success: Focus on the effort you're putting in, not just the end result. Every little bit of progress is a victory.

4. Be Persistent: Remember, even the most beautiful gardens take time to grow. Keep watering and tending to your mindset, and you'll see amazing results.

Interactive Exercise: Mindset Quiz

Let's have a bit of fun with a quick quiz to see where your mindset currently stands. Grab a pen and paper (or use the notes app on your phone), and answer these questions honestly:

1. When faced with a challenge, I...

a) Give up easily.

b) Whine about it but eventually try.

c) See it as a chance to learn and grow.

d) Laugh hysterically and dive right in.

2. When I make a mistake, I...

a) Feel like a failure.

b) Blame the universe and eat ice cream.

c) Look for ways to improve and do better next time.

d) High-five myself for trying and plan my next move.

3. When I see someone who is better than me at something, I...

a) Feel jealous and inadequate.

b) Stalk them on social media and sulk.

c) Feel inspired and motivated to improve.

d) Challenge them to a friendly competition and take notes.

4. When I receive criticism, I...

a) Take it personally and get defensive.

b) Nod politely while plotting revenge.

c) Consider it and use it to grow.

d) Thank the person and ask for more tips.

Scoring

Mostly a's: Fixed Mindset Field. It's time to start pulling those weeds!

Mostly b's: Mixed Mindset Meadow. You're on the right track, but there's room for improvement.

Mostly c's: Growth Mindset Garden. You're cultivating a beautiful space for growth!

Mostly d's: Mindset Master! Your garden is thriving and inspiring everyone around you.

Story: The Tale of Two Students

Let me tell you a story about two students, Jane and John. Jane had a fixed mindset. When she struggled with math, she thought, "I'm just not good at this," and gave up. Her grades were rockier than a mountain goat's path. John, on the other hand, had a growth mindset. He saw his struggles as a chance to learn. He sought help, practiced diligently, and over time, his grades improved. By the end of the semester, John was not only excelling in math but also enjoying it!

Practical Exercise: Mindset Reframe

Here's a little exercise to start shifting your mindset:

1. Identify a Fixed Mindset Thought: Write down a negative thought you've had recently. (e.g., "I'll never be good at public speaking.")

2. Reframe It: Turn that negative thought into a growth mindset statement. (e.g., "I'm not great at public speaking yet, but I can improve with practice.")

3. Take Action: What's one small step you can take to start improving in that area? (e.g., joining a public speaking club or practicing in front of friends.)

Wrap-Up

Your mindset is your mental garden, and you have the power to cultivate it. By embracing a growth mindset, you open yourself up to endless possibilities and set the stage for personal and professional growth. In the next chapter, we'll dive into one of the most powerful tools for mindset transformation: mirror work. So, grab your gardening gloves, and let's get ready to plant some seeds of positivity!

CHAPTER 3
MIRROR, MIRROR ON THE WALL

Get ready for some serious self-reflection—literally. We're about to dive into the world of mirror work. Yes, you heard that right. It's time to have a heart-to-heart with your own reflection. It might sound a bit odd at first, but trust me, this practice can be a game-changer. So, grab your mirrors, and let's get started!

What is Mirror Work?

Mirror work is the practice of looking deeply into your own eyes and speaking positive affirmations out loud. Think of it as a daily pep talk with your best friend—who just so happens to be you. It's a powerful way to boost your self-esteem, reduce negative self-talk, and cultivate a positive self-image. Plus, it's a fantastic way to practice those funny faces you make when nobody's watching.

The Science Behind Mirror Work

You might be wondering, "Isn't this just a bit... vain?" Actually, no! When you look into a mirror and speak kindly to yourself, you're rewiring your brain. Studies have shown that positive affirmations can reduce stress, improve mood, and increase overall well-being (Cohen et al., 2009). It's like giving your brain a warm, fuzzy hug.

How to Practice Mirror Work

Ready to give it a try? Here's a step-by-step guide to help you get started:

1. Find a Mirror: Any mirror will do, but one where you can comfortably see your entire face is ideal. Avoid the funhouse variety unless you want to add a layer of humor to the practice.

2. Get Comfortable: Stand or sit in front of the mirror. Take a few deep breaths and relax. This is your time, so make it as comfortable as possible.

3. Say "I Love You": Start by looking into your eyes and saying, "I love you." It might feel a bit awkward at first, but it's a crucial step. You deserve love from yourself as much as anyone else.

4. Speak Positive Affirmations: Choose a few affirmations that resonate with you. Here are some examples to get you started:

- "I am worthy of love and respect."

- "I am capable of achieving my goals."

- "I love and accept myself exactly as I am."

5. Repeat Daily: Consistency is key. Try to practice mirror work every day, even if it's just for a few minutes. Over time, you'll start to notice a shift in your mindset.

Story: The Shy Superhero

Let me tell you a story about one of my clients, Jake. Jake was a quiet guy who struggled with confidence, feeling unsure of himself in many situations. He dreaded speaking up at work and felt invisible in social situations. I suggested he try mirror work, and though he was skeptical, he gave it a shot. Every morning, Jake looked into his bathroom mirror, said, "I love you," and told himself, "I am confident. I have a powerful voice." It felt silly at first, but after a few weeks, something amazing happened. Jake started speaking up more at work, and his coworkers began to notice his ideas. He even asked someone out on a date! Jake's confidence soared, all thanks to those daily pep talks.

Practical Exercise: Create Your Own Affirmations

Now it's your turn. Let's create some personalized affirmations to use in your mirror work practice. Here's how:

1. Identify Your Goals: What do you want to achieve? More confidence? Greater self-love? Jot down a few goals.

2. Craft Your Affirmations: Turn those goals into positive, present-tense statements. For example:

Goal: To feel more confident in social situations.

Affirmation: "I am confident and comfortable in social settings."

3. Write Them Down: Keep a list of your affirmations where you can see them daily. This will remind you to practice and keep those positive vibes flowing.

4. Start Small: If the idea of talking to yourself in the mirror feels too weird, start with just one affirmation. As you get more comfortable, you can add more.

Fun with Mirrors: Adding Humor to the Mix

Mirror work doesn't have to be all serious. In fact, adding a bit of humor can make the practice even more enjoyable. Try making funny faces at yourself after your affirmations or giving yourself a high-five in the mirror. The goal is to create a positive, uplifting experience that you look forward to each day.

Wrap-Up

Mirror work is a powerful tool for boosting your confidence and transforming your mindset. It might feel a bit silly at first, but stick with it. Remember, the person staring back at you is your biggest supporter. In the next chapter, we'll explore another fantastic tool: written affirmations. So, keep that mirror handy and get ready to write your way to a better mindset!

CHAPTER 4
THE ART OF AFFIRMATION: POWER IN THE PEN

Having polished our reflective skills with mirrors, we're now setting our sights on another transformative tool: written affirmations. These aren't just words on paper; they're declarations of your future victories. So, grab your pen and get ready to write your way to success!

What Are Written Affirmations?

Think of written affirmations as the nutrients for your mental garden. They nurture your thoughts, helping you weed out the negative and fertilize the positive. Written affirmations are those positive phrases you pen down to quiet the inner heckler and amplify your inner cheerleader.

The Power of Putting Pen to Paper

Why write? It's simple: your brain believes what it sees. Writing your affirmations makes them tangible proofs for your skeptical brain, turning whimsical wishes into believable beliefs. It's akin to setting your intentions in stone—or at least in ink.

Crafting Your Affirmations

Mixing the right affirmation cocktail requires a few key ingredients:

1. Keep It Positive: Always use positive phrasing. Switch "I don't do poorly in meetings" to "I excel in meetings."

2. Present Tense Power: State your affirmations in the present tense. Say, "I am," not "I will be." It tricks your brain into thinking the change is already underway.

3. Plausible Promises: Your brain can spot a tall tale. Make sure your affirmations are a stretch but still within the realm of possibility.

4. Pinpoint Precision: The more specific your affirmations, the better. "I am persuasive in discussions" is fine, but "I influence my team positively in every meeting" really hits the mark.

Story: Liz's Career Transformation

Consider Liz, who initially mocked affirmations as "wishful thinking on paper." To prove a point, she began writing, "I am a leader in my field," every morning. As weeks turned into months, Liz noticed real changes: she was more assertive in meetings, her ideas were implemented more frequently, and she was invited to lead bigger projects. Each affirmation acted like a seed, growing her confidence and presence at work. By year's end, she was promoted up two positions with a massive raise—proof that her 'fairy tales' were, in fact, powerful spells for success.

• • •

Practical Exercise: Your Affirmation Station

Here's how you can integrate affirmations into your daily routine:

1. Create a Special Notebook: Call it your Affirmation Journal, a place where you script your ambitions.

2. Daily Dose: Each morning, jot down three affirmations related to your daily goals.

3. Evening Encore: Reflect on these affirmations at night. Notice how they manifested in your day and reinforce your belief in their power.

Laugh Your Way to Change

Inject a bit of humor into your affirmations to keep the vibe light and engaging. Scientific studies have shown that laughter can reduce stress, improve mood, and even boost creativity. So why not make your affirmations a source of joy? Write something like, "I am the wizard of workflow" or "I tackle challenges like a ninja handles missions—efficiently and with a touch of flair."

Wrap-Up

Affirmations are your mental tools for sculpting the life you desire. They're simple, effective, and when infused with a touch of humor, immensely enjoyable. Next up, we'll delve into visualization—where your affirmations leap off the page and into your mind's eye. Prepare to turn your written words into your reality!

CHAPTER 5
VISUALIZATION: CRAFTING YOUR FUTURE WITH A MIND'S EYE

By now, hopefully, you're a master of affirmations, and now we're stepping up our game with visualization. This isn't just make-believe; it's a rehearsal for your success, where the only limit is the boundary of your imagination. Ready to paint the canvas of your future? Let's add some color to those dreams.

What is Visualization?

Think of visualization as your mind's own sketch pad. Here, you're not just daydreaming; you're strategically crafting detailed and dynamic mental images of what you want to achieve. It's like creating your personal highlight reel before the game has even started.

The Science Behind the Scenes

When you vividly imagine achieving your goals, your brain gears up as if you're actually living those achievements, a concept supported by the science of neuroplasticity (Doidge, 2007).

Your brain's neural pathways strengthen as they rehearse your success, priming you for when it's showtime. Essentially, you're tricking your brain into pre-celebrating your victories, which is a great way to ensure it doesn't drop the ball when it matters.

Step-by-Step Visualization

Here's how to bring your mental images to life:

1. Find Your Focus: Settle into a quiet spot where you can concentrate. This is the VIP lounge of your mind—no interruptions allowed.

2. Relax and Ground Yourself: Start with a few deep breaths to clear the stage. It's hard to visualize your triumphs if you're mentally replaying a stressful email or that weird dream from last night.

3. Picture Your Success: Envision your goal in high-definition detail. Imagine the actions, the environment, and even the conversations. If you're aiming for a promotion, see yourself leading meetings and contributing new ideas that are met with nods and applause.

4. Engage Your Senses: What does success smell like? If it's a new job, maybe it's the crisp scent of fresh paper or that new office furniture smell. What sounds accompany this image? The buzz of a busy office, the clink of coffee cups?

5. Embrace the Emotion: How do you feel in this moment of success? Let those feelings be as vivid as the visual details. Happiness, pride, relief—savor them as if they're already yours.

. . .

Lighter Side: When Visualizations Get Playful

Sometimes, the scenes we set in our mind's eye take a playful turn. You might visualize giving a flawless presentation, and your brain decides to add a funny twist—like picturing the audience giving you a standing ovation with confetti raining down. These mental bloopers not only add a laugh but remind us that even in our most carefully crafted visions, it's okay to have a little fun.

Daily Visualization Practice

Make this a part of your daily routine:

1. Morning Preview: Spend a few minutes each morning visualizing a key success of the day. It's like mentally rehearsing for a big game, except the only sweat involved is the effort of your imagination.

2. Midday Mental Check-In: Take a quick mental break to reaffirm your morning's visualization. It's like a sneak peek at your daily highlight reel.

3. Evening Review: At night, reflect on the visualization and the day's events. How closely did reality match your rehearsal? This isn't just daydreaming; it's strategic planning with your eyes closed.

Wrap-Up

Visualization is a powerful tool in your mental toolkit, blending creativity with practicality. It's about setting the stage for your successes and living up to your own hype. Keep it vivid, keep it real, and let your mind do the heavy lifting today for a lighter load tomorrow.

CHAPTER 6
BREATHWORK: MASTERING THE ART OF BREATHING

As we continue our journey into the tools that enhance your mental and emotional well-being, let's take a deep dive into breathwork. This isn't just about taking a breather; it's about mastering your respiratory rhythms to unlock a sense of calm and control. Ready to inhale calm and exhale chaos? Let's learn how.

What is Breathwork?

Breathwork refers to various breathing exercises or techniques that you consciously alter your breathing pattern with. It's a direct way to influence your autonomic nervous system, helping you manage stress, enhance relaxation, and boost your mental clarity.

The Science of Controlled Breathing

Controlled breathing is more than an old wives' tale. It directly impacts your nervous system, reducing stress hormones, improving oxygen delivery, and even helping regulate your heart rate and digestion. Basically, mastering your breath can make you the master of your mood.

Techniques to Try

Let's focus on two foundational techniques that are simple yet profoundly impactful:

3-3-3 Breathing Technique: This involves breathing in deeply through your nose for 3 seconds, holding that breath for 3 seconds, and then exhaling slowly through your mouth for 3 seconds. It's a quick and effective method to center yourself, especially useful when stress levels start to rise. Think of it as a mini reset button you can press anytime you need a moment of calm.

4-4-4 Energizing Breath Walk: For a more invigorating practice, try this. While walking, inhale through your nose for 4 seconds. Hold that breath for 4 seconds, then exhale through your mouth for 4 seconds. Hold your breath for another 4 seconds before starting the cycle again.

To add rhythm and enhance focus, tap your fingers together on each hand in a sequence—thumb to pointer, thumb to middle, thumb to ring, and thumb to pinky—both hands at the same time. This can create a tactile rhythm that complements your breathing pattern.

Picture yourself walking at a comfortable pace, breathing in a steady rhythm, and tapping your fingers in sync. This technique not only reduces stress but also boosts energy, improves concentration, and keeps your body and mind engaged. It's perfect for when you need a pick-me-up during the day or a mental reset between tasks.

Wrap-Up

Both of these techniques offer unique benefits. The 3-3-3 Breathing Technique provides a quick, calming reset, while the 4-4-4 Energizing Breath Walk adds a rhythmic, invigorating boost to your routine. Try incorporating both into your day to see which works best for different situations.

Story: Breathwork in Daily Life: Anna's Story

Meet Anna, a competitive cyclist who used the 3-3-3 breathing technique to enhance her focus and performance during races. Initially, Anna struggled with pre-race jitters that impacted her stamina and speed. By integrating the 3-3-3 technique into her pre-race routine, she found she could better regulate her heart rate and calm her nerves. This simple change helped her maintain a clearer focus throughout her races, leading to improved times and a more enjoyable racing experience.

Integrating Breathwork Into Your Routine

Here's how you can seamlessly incorporate these techniques into your daily life:

1. Morning Energizer: Start your day with the 4-4-4 Energizing Breath Walk. Walk at a comfortable pace, inhale for 4 seconds, hold for 4 seconds, exhale for 4 seconds, and hold again for 4 seconds. Tap your fingers together—thumb to pointer, thumb to middle, and so on—to create a rhythmic pattern that keeps your mind engaged and your energy levels up.

2. Midday Moment: Use the 3-3-3 Breathing Technique to reset and refocus your energy. Inhale for 3 seconds, hold for 3 seconds, and exhale for 3 seconds. This can be done during a lunch break or between meetings for a quick mental cleanse.

3. Evening Wind-Down: Before bed, use the 3-3-3 Breathing Technique to help signal to your body that it's time to slow down and prepare for sleep, washing away the stress of the day. Inhale for 3 seconds, hold for 3 seconds, and exhale for 3 seconds.

Wrap-Up

Breathwork is an essential tool in your wellness toolkit, providing a simple yet effective way to enhance your daily life. Whether you're gearing up for a stressful event or winding down after a long day, these breathing techniques can offer immediate relief and lasting benefits. Embrace the power of your breath and transform the way you respond to life's challenges.

CHAPTER 7
MEDITATION FOR MINDSET

Now that you're becoming a breathwork pro, let's dive into the world of meditation. Think of meditation not just as a way to find quiet, but as a personal brain gym where your mind gets to learn focus and resilience. Whether you're looking to escape the daily grind or sharpen your mental clarity, these techniques can be tailored to fit your needs. Let's explore this journey together.

What is Meditation?

Meditation is the art of focusing the mind, reducing mental noise, and promoting deep personal growth. It's like giving your brain a spa day, training it to focus and redirect thoughts, enhancing overall mental well-being, and reducing stress.

The Science of Silence

Research shows that meditation can help reduce stress, control anxiety, improve emotional health, and enhance attention. It's a mental exercise that strengthens your brain's ability to concentrate and stay calm under pressure. Imagine being able to handle life's curveballs with the grace of a zen master—sounds good, right?

Core Meditation Techniques

Let's explore two fundamental meditation techniques, now with a touch of fun—using a nonsense word or focusing on ambient sounds.

1. Mindfulness Meditation:

Setting Up: Find a quiet spot where you can sit or lie down comfortably. Use a cushion, chair, or any spot that gives you a stable, comfortable posture. Think of it as creating your own little sanctuary of peace.

The Practice: Close your eyes and take a few deep breaths to relax. Choose a focus for your meditation: this could be your breath, a nonsense word (like "shoom" or "blemp"), or an ambient sound (like the ticking of a clock or the distant hum of traffic). Let this be the anchor of your attention. When your **mind** wanders, gently bring your focus back. No judgment—just a gentle nudge.

Duration: Start with about five minutes per day. Gradually increase the duration as you become more comfortable with the practice. You're not training for the meditation Olympics—take your time!

2. Guided Meditation:

Finding a Guide: Select a guided meditation from an app or online that resonates with you. Many apps offer sessions focused on different anchors for attention.

The Practice: Use headphones to help focus and follow the guidance provided. The narrator might lead you through visualizations or focus exercises using the sound of their voice or other auditory cues.

Consistency: Regular practice is key, even if it's just a few minutes each day. Experiment with different guided meditations to find what works best for you. Think of it as dating different meditation styles until you find "the one."

Integrating Meditation into Your Daily Life

Here's how you can seamlessly incorporate these techniques throughout your day:

1. Morning Energizer: Start your day with the 4-4-4 Energizing Breath Walk. Walk at a comfortable pace, inhale for 4 seconds, hold for 4 seconds, exhale for 4 seconds, and hold again for 4 seconds. Tap your fingers together—thumb to pointer, thumb to middle, and so on—to create a rhythmic pattern that keeps your mind engaged and your energy levels up.

2. Midday Moment: Use the 3-3-3 Breathing Technique to reset and refocus your energy. Inhale for 3 seconds, hold for 3 seconds, and exhale for 3 seconds. This can be done during a lunch break or between meetings for a quick mental cleanse.

3. Evening Wind-Down: Before bed, use the 3-3-3 Breathing Technique to help signal to your body that it's time to slow down and prepare for sleep, washing away the stress of the day. Inhale for 3 seconds, hold for 3 seconds, and exhale for 3 seconds.

Story: Meditation Magic—Sarah's Transformation

Meet Sarah, a busy marketing executive who felt like she was always running on empty. Between work deadlines and family commitments, she hardly had a moment to herself. One day, a friend suggested she try meditation. Skeptical but desperate, Sarah decided to give it a shot.

She started with the 4-4-4 Energizing Breath Walk in the mornings. Walking through her neighborhood, she inhaled for 4 seconds, held for 4 seconds, exhaled for 4 seconds, and held again for 4 seconds, tapping her fingers together rhythmically. It felt a bit silly at first, but she quickly noticed how it energized her and set a positive tone for the day. Her morning anxiety diminished, and she felt more prepared to tackle her tasks.

During lunch breaks, she used the 3-3-3 Breathing Technique to reset. Sitting quietly at her desk, she would inhale for 3 seconds, hold for 3 seconds, and exhale for 3 seconds. This short practice became her midday oasis, helping her regain focus and calm. Her afternoon productivity soared, and she found herself less overwhelmed by her workload.

At night, she spent a few minutes in mindfulness meditation. She chose a nonsense word, "shoom," and whenever her mind wandered, she gently brought it back. This practice helped her unwind and sleep better. Within weeks, Sarah noticed significant changes. She felt more balanced, her stress levels decreased, and she approached challenges with newfound clarity.

Meditation became her secret weapon, transforming her hectic life into a more manageable and enjoyable experience. She even found that her relationships improved as she became more present and less reactive.

Wrap-Up

Meditation is a versatile and powerful tool for enhancing your mental clarity and emotional balance. By practicing regularly and focusing on techniques that work best for you —be it breath, a nonsense word, or a consistent ambient sound—you build a strong foundation for mental health and well-being. Each session is an opportunity to cultivate peace and resilience, paving the way for a more mindful and focused life.

CHAPTER 8
EVIDENCE LISTS: CELEBRATING SMALL WINS

It's time to focus on a powerful yet often overlooked tool: evidence lists. Think of them as my version of a gratitude journal. This simple technique involves recording your daily successes and positive experiences, helping you build a solid foundation of confidence and positivity. Ready to start recognizing and celebrating every victory, no matter how small? Let's dive in!

What are Evidence Lists?

Evidence lists are essentially a form of journaling, but instead of writing about your day in general, you specifically note down achievements, positive outcomes, or any progress made toward your goals. It's like collecting pieces of evidence to prove to yourself that yes, you are making strides and improving, even when it doesn't feel like it. With my clients, we like to use it as 'evidence' that all of the mindset and energy work they are doing is creating big and small miracles in their lives, and they have the records to prove it!

· · ·

The Power of Positive Recording

Maintaining an evidence list has profound psychological benefits. It helps combat negativity bias—the brain's tendency to remember negative experiences more vividly than positive ones. By regularly noting down positive experiences, you're training your brain to focus on the good, which can enhance your overall mental health, increase resilience, and boost your happiness. Doing this at the end of the day will get your brain in 'positive mode,' setting you up for a great night's sleep and a fantastic start to the next day.

As you wire new positive neurons in your brain, these neurons become little detectives. The more you focus on positive experiences, the more you create that focus. You will begin to consciously and subconsciously look for 'evidence' of good things in your day.

How to Create an Effective Evidence List

Creating an evidence list doesn't have to be a chore. Here's how to make it a rewarding part of your daily routine:

1. Choose Your Medium: Decide whether you prefer a digital note on your phone or a physical notebook dedicated to your evidence list. Each has its benefits: digital is always with you, while writing by hand can be more reflective. (I strongly urge you to lean toward writing it. There is evidence of the greater strength in the mind/body connection when writing and wiring our brain for new thinking).

2. Set a Daily Reminder: Consistency is key. Set a specific time each day to update your evidence list. It could be during your morning coffee, your lunch break, or right before bed. (I always urge my clients to do this right before bed—as the very last thing they do before falling asleep. But anytime you can get it in is better than not doing it at all!).

3. Be Specific and Varied: Include a variety of positives. It could be a compliment received, a task completed, or even a moment where you felt peaceful. The more specific you are, the more vividly you'll remember these moments.

4. Reflect Weekly: Once a week, take some time to review your list. This reflection can provide a tremendous emotional uplift and give you a clear picture of your weekly accomplishments.

Integrating Evidence Lists Into Your Life

Here are some tips to seamlessly integrate evidence lists into your daily life:

1. Morning Motivation: Start your day by reading a few past entries. This can provide motivation and set a positive tone for the day ahead.

2. Lunchtime Look-back: Use a few minutes of your lunch break to jot down positive experiences from the morning.

3. Evening Review: Before bed, reflect on the day and write down any successes or positive moments. This practice can help end your day on a positive note, promoting better sleep.

Story: Emma's Transformation

Meet Emma, a professor who felt overwhelmed by the daily grind and often struggled to see the positives in her hectic schedule. Emma started using an evidence list after one of our sessions. She decided to dedicate a small notebook to this practice and kept it by her bedside table.

Initially, Emma wrote simple entries like, "Finished grading papers on time," or "Had a nice chat with a colleague." But as she continued, her entries became more meaningful: "A student thanked me for helping them understand a tough concept," and "Felt a sense of peace during my lunchtime walk."

After a month, Emma noticed a significant shift in her mindset. She felt more optimistic and resilient. Her evenings were less stressful, and she began to sleep better. Reviewing her evidence list each night helped her end the day on a high note, appreciating the small wins that often went unnoticed before. This simple habit transformed her outlook, making her more present and engaged in her daily life.

Wrap-Up

Evidence lists are a simple yet powerful tool to enhance your awareness of life's positives. My favorite way to engage with this practice is right before bed, as the last thing I do each day. This timing isn't just about convenience—it's strategic. By focusing on your successes and moments of joy at night, you prime your sleeping consciousness to operate from a place of gratitude and positivity. This practice can influence the tone of your dreams and the quality of your rest, setting a positive tone for the following day.

As you continue to use this tool, you'll likely find that your days are richer and your perspective brighter than you ever realized. The act of writing down positive experiences consistently helps build a habit of positivity that can transform your overall outlook on life and deeply ingrain a sense of accomplishment and happiness in your psyche.

CHAPTER 9
CREATING AN ENERGY FIELD: CULTIVATING YOUR PERSONAL SPACE

Let's explore a critical aspect of personal development through energy—creating and maintaining a positive energy field. This chapter will guide you through the process of shaping an energy field that protects and enhances your personal space. Ready to weave a shield of positivity around yourself? Let's begin.

What is an Energy Field?

Your energy field, or "aura," is an electromagnetic layer that surrounds your body, mirroring your emotional, mental, and spiritual state. This personal bubble interacts with the world around you, influencing and being influenced by other energies. Managing this field actively can help you shape how you experience and impact your surroundings.

The Science Behind Energy Fields

Energy fields may seem mystical, but they are underpinned by the electromagnetic fields all living beings generate. These fields are intertwined with our psychological and physiological states, influencing everything from mood swings to social interactions.

Techniques to Enhance Your Energy Field

To nurture a vibrant energy field, consider these practices:

1. Regular Cleansing: Engage in activities that clear your energy field, like meditation, nature walks, or smudging with sage or palo santo.

2. Visualization for Protection: Regularly visualize your energy field as a strong, clear shield, warding off negativity and drawing in positivity.

3. Setting Daily Intentions: Each morning, set a clear intention to fortify your energy field, helping you attract the experiences and interactions you desire.

4. Crystals for Energy Enhancement: Incorporate crystals like quartz or amethyst into your routine to support and strengthen your energy field.

Guided Visualization for Energy Protection

Let's dive into a specific guided visualization to enhance your energy field:

1. Find a Quiet Space: Sit or lie down in a quiet, comfortable place where you won't be disturbed.

2. Relax Your Body: Close your eyes and take several deep breaths. With each exhale, let go of any tension or stress in your body.

3. Visualize Protective Light: Imagine a bright light—warm and soothing—emanating from the core of your body. Visualize this light expanding slowly, enveloping you in a sphere of radiant energy.

4. Choose Your Shape: As the light surrounds you, shape it into a form that resonates with you—a sphere, a cube, a pyramid, or any other shape that feels protective. See this shape as a strong, clear boundary that shields you.

5. Set the Intention of Love: Focus on the intent that this protective shape allows only love and positivity to enter and exit. It filters out any negativity, leaving only what serves your highest good.

6. Hold the Visualization: Maintain this visualization for a few minutes, reinforcing the strength and clarity of your protective shape. Feel the peace and security that it provides.

7. Gently Return: When you're ready, slowly bring your awareness back to your surroundings. Take a few deep breaths, and when you open your eyes, carry the sense of protection and calm with you.

Story: Alexander's Awakening

Meet Alexander, a successful entrepreneur and philanthropist who always felt a higher calling to make a difference in the world. Despite his achievements, he often felt drained and overwhelmed by the demands of his high-stakes career and numerous charitable projects.

Alexander came to me seeking a way to manage his energy and protect his well-being amidst his hectic life. During our sessions, I introduced him to the concept of creating an energy field. Curious, he decided to give it a try. Each morning, before diving into his busy schedule, Alexander would sit quietly in his home office. He imagined a bright, golden light emanating from his heart, slowly expanding to form a protective bubble around him. This bubble, he envisioned, would shield him from negativity and stress while attracting positivity and peace.

As his days unfolded, whenever Alexander felt the pressures of work or the weight of responsibility, he would pause for a moment to reinforce his protective bubble. He even started carrying a small piece of quartz in his pocket as a physical reminder of his energy shield.

Within a few weeks, Alexander noticed profound changes. He felt more grounded and less susceptible to the chaos around him. His interactions with colleagues and partners became more harmonious, and he approached challenges with a newfound sense of calm and clarity. The energy he used to spend on stress and worry was now channeled into his passion projects and philanthropic efforts.

Creating and maintaining his energy field became Alexander's secret weapon, enabling him to fulfill his higher calling with greater ease and joy. His life transformed from a constant struggle to a balanced flow of productivity and fulfillment.

Daily Practices to Maintain Your Energy Field

Incorporate these steps into your daily routine to keep your energy field vibrant:

1. Morning Activation: Start each day by reactivating the protective shape around you through a quick visualization.

2. Mindful Monitoring: Throughout the day, stay mindful of your energy. If you sense disturbances, take a moment to visualize reinforcing your protective shape.

3. Evening Cleanse: Before bed, visualize any accumulated negative energy dissolving away, leaving your protective shape clear and strong.

Wrap-Up

Maintaining a positive energy field is a dynamic and rewarding practice that enhances your physical, emotional, and spiritual well-being. By regularly visualizing protection and setting intentions, you create a personal space that supports your growth and happiness.

CHAPTER 10
INTENTION SETTING: YOUR DAILY BLUEPRINT FOR SUCCESS

Let's switch gears and dive into intention setting. Think of this as your daily to-do list, but instead of mundane tasks like "buy milk" or "file reports," you're listing epic life goals like "radiate positivity" or "conquer fears." Ready to map out a day that could make even superheroes envious? Let's set some powerful intentions!

What is Intention Setting?

Intention setting is the art of defining a clear, positive focus before you start your day. It's like programming your GPS with the destination "Best Day Ever" each morning. This practice helps steer your actions and mindset, ensuring that your daily journey aligns with your broader life goals.

The Science of Setting Intentions

Science backs up the power of intention setting. Studies show that when we start our day with a clear focus, we're more productive, less prone to distraction, and more resilient to stress. It's like setting the thermostat of your mood; get it right in the morning, and the whole day heats up with potential.

Techniques to Master Intention Setting

Setting intentions doesn't have to be a solemn ritual—it can be as fun and creative as you make it. Here are some techniques to get you started:

1. Morning Meditation: Incorporate a short meditation session into your morning routine where you visualize your day going exactly as you intend. Imagine everything from nailing presentations to having peaceful coffee breaks.

2. Write It Down: Grab a notepad and jot down your intentions. Writing helps solidify thoughts in your mind—it's like signing a contract with yourself to have an amazing day.

3. Use Affirmations: Craft a few positive affirmations that align with your intentions. Repeating statements like "I am focused and serene under pressure" can prime your brain to make it a reality.

Daily Practice of Intention Setting

Integrating intention setting into your daily routine can be straightforward and immensely rewarding:

1. Kickstart Your Day: Before you even roll out of bed, spend a few minutes setting your intentions. Think of it as loading the right software for the day.

2. Lunchtime Review: Midday, revisit your intentions. It's a great checkpoint to see if your day is on course or needs a slight recalibration.

3. Evening Reflection: At night, reflect on how well your intentions aligned with your day's events. It's like checking the score at the end of a game and planning strategies for the next match.

Wrap-Up

Intention setting is not just about wishing how your day goes; it's about actively crafting the framework on which your day builds. With each intention, you lay down a brick in the construction of your life. Remember, the power of intention is only as strong as the humor and joy you infuse into it. So set your intentions, but don't forget to laugh when things go awry—it's all part of the journey.

CHAPTER 11
SEGMENTING YOUR DAY: MASTERING TRANSITIONS WITH A SMILE

It's time to tackle time management—but not in the boring old way you might expect. Think of day segmenting as the art of mastering life's transitions, much like a stand-up comic knows exactly when to deliver a punchline for maximum effect. Ready to optimize your day with strategic transitions? Let's map out your routine with a twist!

What is Day Segmenting?

Think of day segmenting as the comedy routine of time management. Just as a good comic masterfully transitions from one joke to another, you'll learn to glide through your day with the same finesse. It's not just about slicing your calendar into pieces; it's about being mindful of the major transitions in your day—like going to work, having lunch, heading home, spending time with family, or going out with friends. By setting a mental intention and incorporating breathwork to reset and create new intended energy for each segment, you bring more awareness and positive energy into your day.

. . .

The Science Behind Effective Segmenting

Why does segmenting work? Studies show that our brains love a good segue as much as an audience loves a killer punchline. By breaking your day into distinct "acts" or segments, you reduce the mental load and give your brain the cue sheets it needs to perform at its best. It's like telling your brain, "Here's what's up next on the agenda!" This helps you be more present and intentional, making each part of your day more effective and enjoyable.

Techniques for Effective Day Segmenting

To master the art of transitioning like a pro, here's how you can effectively segment your day:

1. Morning Routine Talk Show: Start your day by hosting a little talk show in your head. Review your day's script—err, schedule—and plan out your segments. It's your show, so you decide the lineup!

2. Curtain Calls and Scene Changes: Use natural breaks—like traveling or finishing a task—as your curtain calls to switch scenes. Each transition is a chance to breathe, reset, and cue up the next part of your performance.

3. Props and Settings: Modify your environment to match your segments. Moving to a café or switching from desk to standing might just be the scene change you need to keep the audience—aka your brain—engaged.

Story: Jessica's Journey

Meet Jessica, a stay-at-home mom who often felt overwhelmed by her daily responsibilities. Her days were filled with caring for her children, managing the household, and trying to find moments for herself. Jessica sought my help to bring more balance and mindfulness into her life.

Together, we identified the key segments of Jessica's day: her morning routine, preparing the kids for school, household chores, lunchtime, afternoon activities with the kids, evening family time, and personal relaxation time. I taught Jessica how to set intentions for each segment and use breathwork to reset her energy.

In the morning, Jessica started her day with a brief meditation and visualization, setting a positive intention for the day. As she prepared her kids for school, she practiced the 3-3-3 Breathing Technique to stay calm and focused.

During her household chores, Jessica used short mindfulness breaks, pausing to take deep breaths and reset her energy. Lunchtime became a moment of reflection and relaxation, where she would take a few minutes to breathe deeply and set intentions for the afternoon.

In the afternoon, Jessica engaged in activities with her kids, setting a clear intention to be present and enjoy their time together. Before transitioning to evening family time, she spent a few minutes visualizing a protective light around her, releasing any stress from the day.

By segmenting her day and setting clear intentions, Jessica felt more in control and less stressed. She was able to be fully present in each part of her day, leading to a more harmonious and enjoyable family life.

Integrating Segmenting into Your Routine

Here's how to make day segmenting a hit show every day:

1. Dynamic Daily Setup: Each morning, script out your day.

Be the director of your own life, setting the stage for what's to come.

2. Curtain Calls: Use natural breaks to transition. For example, your commute or a coffee break can be a moment to reset and prepare for the next segment.

3. Mindful Monitoring: Throughout the day, stay aware of your energy. If you sense disturbances, take a moment to reset using breathwork.

4. Evening Review: At the end of the day, review your performance. Reflect on what worked well and where you can improve.

Example: A Day in Segments

Morning:

- **Intention:** Start the day with positivity and focus.
- **Action:** Meditate for 5 minutes, set daily goals.
- **Breathwork:** 3-3-3 Breathing Technique during morning routine.

Kids to School:

- **Intention:** Stay calm and organized.
- **Action:** Prepare breakfast, help kids get ready.
- **Breathwork:** Deep breaths to maintain calm.

Household Chores:

- **Intention:** Complete tasks efficiently.
- **Action:** Tackle chores one by one.
- **Breathwork:** Short mindfulness breaks between tasks.

Lunch:

- **Intention:** Recharge and relax.
- **Action:** Enjoy lunch without distractions.
- **Breathwork:** Deep breathing exercises to reset.

Afternoon Activities:

- **Intention:** Be present and engaged.
- **Action:** Play and interact with kids.
- **Breathwork:** Deep breaths to stay centered.

Evening:

- **Intention:** Relax and enjoy family time.
- **Action:** Dinner, family activities.
- **Breathwork:** Visualization and breathing to release stress.

Night:

- **Intention:** Wind down and prepare for restful sleep.
- **Action:** Reflect on the day, write in your evidence list.
- **Breathwork:** Gentle breathing exercises to promote relaxation.

Wrap-Up

Mastering day segmenting with a sense of mindfulness allows you to manage your time effectively while enjoying each part of your day. It turns routine into a series of intentional acts, and transitions into opportunities to reset and refocus. With this approach, not only are you productive, but you're also more aware and engaged—and isn't that the best way to play the game of life?

CHAPTER 12
FINDING YOUR INNER GLOW

We've talked about affirmations, meditation, and breathwork, but now it's time to get a bit more mystical. Let's dive into connecting with your inner, divine light—think of it as finding your personal lighthouse guiding you through the fog. Ready to shine bright like a diamond? Let's illuminate the way!

Understanding Your Inner, Divine Light

Your inner, divine light is the essence of your true self—your secret sauce, your personal superpower. It's that spark that makes you uniquely you. Connecting with this light helps you align with your true self, like finding the perfect playlist that just gets you.

Why Connecting to Your Inner Light is Important

1. Inner Peace: Tapping into your inner light is like having a built-in spa day for your soul.

2. Guidance: It's your personal GPS, helping you navigate life's twists and turns without needing a map (or asking for directions).

3. Empowerment: Embracing your inner light is like wearing an invisible superhero cape. Suddenly, you're unstoppable.

Techniques to Connect with Your Inner, Divine Light

Here are some fun and effective ways to connect with your inner glow:

1. Meditation: Think of meditation as your personal zen garden. Sit comfortably, close your eyes, and imagine your inner light as a glowing orb. Let it shine brighter with each breath.

2. Affirmations: Use affirmations that make you feel like the star you are. Try, "I am a radiant being of light" or "My inner light guides me with clarity and wisdom."

3. Journaling: Grab your favorite pen and start scribbling about times when you felt truly yourself. Reflect on those moments and brainstorm how to invite more of that into your life.

4. Nature Walks: Nature is like Mother Earth's free therapy session. Go for a walk, breathe deeply, and let the natural beauty remind you of your own inner brilliance.

5. Creative Expression: Whether it's doodling, dancing, or playing the ukulele, let your creative juices flow. Creativity is a direct hotline to your true self.

Guided Visualization for Connecting with Your Inner Light

Here's a playful guided visualization to help you connect with your inner light:

1. Find a Quiet Space: Sit or lie down somewhere comfy—think of it as your cozy cocoon.

2. Relax Your Body: Close your eyes and take a few deep breaths. Imagine melting into a puddle of relaxation.

3. Visualize a Light: Picture a warm, glowing light at the center of your being. This is your inner light, your personal disco ball.

4. Expand the Light: Visualize this light expanding, filling your entire body with its glow. Feel the warmth spreading like a cozy blanket.

5. Embrace the Light: Bask in this light for a few minutes. Feel it guiding you, like a lighthouse in a storm.

6. Return with Clarity: Slowly bring your awareness back to the room. Open your eyes and take a few more deep breaths, feeling refreshed and ready to dazzle.

Story: David's Discovery

Meet David, a software engineer who often felt disconnected from his work and life. Despite his technical skills and professional success, he yearned for a deeper connection to his true self and a sense of fulfillment beyond his career.

Application of the Tool:

David came to me looking for ways to reconnect with his inner light. We began with daily meditation sessions. Each morning, David would sit quietly in his home office, close his eyes, and visualize a warm, glowing light at the center of his being. He imagined this light expanding with each breath, filling his entire body and radiating outward.

David also started using affirmations. He would begin his day by saying, "I am a radiant being of light" and "My inner light guides me with clarity and wisdom." These affirmations helped him feel more aligned with his true self and set a positive tone for the day.

To further deepen his connection, David took up journaling. He reflected on moments when he felt most authentic and brainstormed ways to invite more of those experiences into his life. Nature walks became a vital part of his routine; the tranquility of the outdoors helped him feel grounded and reminded him of his own inner brilliance.

David also rediscovered his love for playing the guitar. He used creative expression as a direct hotline to his true self, allowing his creativity to flow freely without judgment.

Outcome:

Over time, David's life began to transform. He felt more connected to his true self and experienced a newfound sense of inner peace. His decisions became more aligned with his values, and he exuded confidence. David found joy in both his professional and personal life, navigating his days with clarity and purpose. His colleagues noticed the positive change, and his renewed energy and enthusiasm even inspired his team. David's journey to connect with his inner light turned him into a beacon of positivity and strength.

Wrap-Up

Connecting with your inner, divine light is like finding your personal north star. It guides you, grounds you, and makes you shine. By incorporating meditation, affirmations, journaling, nature walks, and creative expression, you can light up your path and live authentically. So go ahead, let your light shine—because the world needs your unique sparkle.

CHAPTER 13
CREATING YOUR PERSONAL ENERGY AND MINDSET CHART: YOUR DAILY ROADMAP TO AWESOME

Let's simplify and supercharge your daily routine by creating a personal energy and mindset chart. This isn't just any chart—it's your daily roadmap to becoming awesomely happy. Think of it as your personal assistant who's always cheerful and a bit too enthusiastic about checklists. Ready to lay out a clear, focused plan for your daily energy and mindset practices? Let's roll up our sleeves (or cape, if you prefer) and get to it!

What is a Personal Energy and Mindset Chart?

Your personal energy and mindset chart is a straightforward, visual tool designed to help you apply the techniques we've explored—like your very own daily game plan. It's like having a cheat sheet for acing the game of life every single day.

Why You Absolutely Need This Chart

1. Consistency is King (or Queen): Regular practice is the secret to seeing results. This chart keeps you honest and consistent.

2. Visual Motivation: Seeing your progress visually is incredibly motivating. It's like watching your fitness progress in the mirror, but for your brain.

3. Simplicity: No more wondering, "What should I do today to boost my mindset?" It's all laid out in your chart, clear as day.

4. It's Fun: Yes, fun! Tracking your daily wins gives you a little dopamine hit, not unlike crossing off items on your to-do list. Who knew self-improvement could be addictive?

Designing Your Chart

Let's keep it simple and effective:

1. Choose Your Daily Tools: Select a few key practices from the book that resonate most with you, such as affirmations, breathwork, or meditation. No need to overdo it—just what feels manageable and impactful.

2. Layout: Create a daily chart with sections for each practice. You can make it colorful, add stickers, or whatever tickles your fancy. Make it a chart you'd want to hang on your fridge!

3. Detailed Instructions: At the bottom or back of the chart, jot down brief instructions or specific phrases for each practice. For example, list your go-to affirmations or outline a quick breathwork routine.

4. Tracking: Include a simple way to track your daily practice, like a checkbox or a smiley face. Every mark represents a step toward a happier you.

Integrating the Chart into Your Routine

1. Morning Ritual: Start your day by reviewing your chart. This sets your intentions and gets you pumped for the day ahead.

2. Evening Review: Spend a few minutes each evening updating your chart. Celebrate your achievements, no matter how small—they all count!

3. Weekly Recap: At the end of the week, give your chart a quick once-over. What worked well? What didn't? Adjust as needed, and prepare to tackle the next week.

Wrap-Up

Creating and using your personal energy and mindset chart isn't just about following a routine—it's about creating a habit that builds a happier, more fulfilled you. It's your daily dose of structure with a side of fun, ensuring that each day you're not just going through the motions, but actively enhancing your life. So, chart your course, check those boxes, and let's make every day a little brighter, one tick at a time!

CHAPTER 14
REAL-LIFE APPLICATIONS: TRANSFORMATIONAL STORIES

Welcome back! Having explored a range of techniques for enhancing mindset and energy, it's time to see how these tools translate into success for individuals in different environments. This chapter delves into the stories of three individuals who effectively integrated these strategies into their lives, achieving remarkable transformations.

Affirmation Mastery: Claudia's Leadership Evolution

Claudia, a CEO of a burgeoning fintech startup, faced immense pressure to lead her company through rapid growth phases. Despite her experience, she often doubted her decisions, feeling the weight of her team's and investors' expectations.

Application of the Tool: Claudia created a weekly "Leadership Confidence Chart" incorporating three key tools: affirmations, visualization, and breathwork.

1. Affirmations: Claudia selected affirmations such as "I am a decisive and effective leader" and "I trust my intuition and make informed decisions." She recited these affirmations each morning and before important meetings.

2. Visualization: Every day, Claudia spent five minutes visualizing her success in upcoming meetings and presentations, picturing herself confidently leading her team.

3. Breathwork: Claudia practiced the 4-4-4 Energizing Breath Walk each morning during her commute to maintain her energy and focus throughout the day.

Claudia's chart included sections for daily affirmations, visualization, and breathwork, with checkboxes to track her consistency and notes to reflect on her progress.

Outcome: Over several months, Claudia's confidence soared. Her decision-making process became more streamlined, and she communicated her vision more effectively. The company secured two major rounds of funding and expanded its market presence. Claudia's story shows how combining affirmations, visualization, and breathwork can enhance self-assurance and clarity in leadership roles.

Mindfulness Meditation: Raj's Turnaround Strategy

Raj, a senior partner at a leading law firm, struggled with burnout and high stress due to the demanding nature of his job. His ability to focus and lead his team effectively was compromised, affecting his performance and personal life.

Application of the Tool: Raj designed a "Stress Management Chart" using three key tools: mindfulness meditation, breathwork, and gratitude practice.

1. Mindfulness Meditation: Raj dedicated 15 minutes each morning to meditate in his office, focusing on breathing techniques and present-moment awareness.

2. Breathwork: Throughout the day, Raj practiced the 3-3-3 Breathing Technique during short breaks to reset his mind and reduce stress.

3. Gratitude Practice: Each evening, Raj wrote down three things he was grateful for, helping him maintain a positive mindset.

Raj's chart included sections for daily meditation, breathwork sessions, and gratitude entries, with checkboxes to track his progress and notes to reflect on his experiences.

Outcome: Raj experienced a profound improvement in his mental clarity and stress management. His meditation practice helped him approach complex cases with a fresh perspective and maintain his poise in stressful negotiations. His leadership saw improved outcomes in trial preparations and client interactions, earning him a reputation for his composed demeanor and sharp focus.

Structured Day Segmenting: Angela's Proactive Planning

Angela, the Director of Operations at a multinational corporation, was overwhelmed by the constant demands of her leadership role, often feeling that her work life bled into her personal time. This not only affected her effectiveness but also her well-being.

Application of the Tool: Angela created a "Productivity and Balance Chart" incorporating three key tools: day segmenting, intention setting, and mirror work.

1. Day Segmenting: Angela reviewed her calendar each morning to identify key transitions and scheduled 5-minute segmenting breaks to reset and refocus.

2. Intention Setting: Angela set clear intentions for each segment of her day, ensuring she approached each task with a fresh perspective and optimal energy.

3. Mirror Work: Each evening, Angela spent a few minutes doing mirror work, looking at herself and saying, "I am proud of what I accomplished today" and "I will rest and rejuvenate for tomorrow."

Angela's chart had sections for daily segmenting breaks, intention setting, and mirror work, with spaces to note her reflections and adjustments.

Outcome: This methodical approach significantly improved Angela's ability to manage her responsibilities. She reported a notable decrease in stress and an increase in productivity, as each segment of her day received her full attention and energy. Her team also benefited from her more focused and calm leadership. Angela's story demonstrates how effective segmenting, intention setting, and mirror work can transform a leader's day from chaotic and reactive to structured and proactive.

Finding Inner Peace: Jessica's Journey

Jessica, a stay-at-home mom, often felt overwhelmed by her daily responsibilities. Despite loving her family, she craved a deeper connection to her true self and a sense of personal fulfillment.

Application of the Tool: Jessica created a "Peace and Presence Chart" using three key tools: energy field creation, affirmations, and creative expression.

1. Energy Field Creation: Each morning, Jessica spent a few minutes visualizing a protective energy field around her, starting her day with a sense of security and calm.

2. Affirmations: Jessica selected affirmations like "I am a beacon of calm and love" and "I nurture myself and my family with patience and joy." She repeated these affirmations during her morning routine and throughout the day.

3. Creative Expression: Jessica set aside time each day to engage in creative activities she loved, such as painting and writing, allowing her to express her true self.

Jessica's chart included sections for daily energy field visualization, affirmations, and creative activities, with checkboxes to track her progress and notes to reflect on her feelings and experiences.

Outcome: Over time, Jessica felt a profound sense of inner peace and fulfillment. She found joy in both the small moments and the larger aspects of her life, navigating her days with clarity and purpose. Her family noticed the positive change, feeling the calm and loving energy she brought into their home. Jessica's story shows how combining energy field creation, affirmations, and creative expression can lead to a balanced and fulfilling life.

Wrap-Up

These stories illustrate just a few ways that energy and mindset techniques can be adapted to suit various life circumstances. Each individual used these tools to forge a path to greater success, showcasing the versatility and impact of applying these strategies in different roles. As you reflect on these examples, consider how you might tailor these techniques to bolster your own journey and drive meaningful change in your professional and personal life.

CONCLUSION: EMBRACE YOUR JOURNEY

Congratulations on making it to the end of this book! You've embarked on a transformative journey, exploring the depths of energy and mindset work. This isn't just a one-time read; it's a guide to continuously refer back to as you navigate the ups and downs of life. Let's wrap up with some final thoughts and encouragement to keep you motivated on your path.

Final Thoughts and Encouragement

Remember, the practices you've learned here are tools to help you build a happier, more fulfilling life. They are your allies in navigating challenges and celebrating triumphs. Consistency is key, but so is kindness to yourself. Some days will be easier than others, and that's perfectly okay.

- **Consistency Over Perfection**: It's not about doing everything perfectly every day. It's about showing up for yourself, even in small ways, consistently.

- **Celebrate Small Wins**: Every step forward, no matter how small, is progress. Celebrate those moments.

- **Stay Curious**: Keep exploring new ways to enhance your energy and mindset. The journey doesn't end here; it's a lifelong adventure.

Recap of Key Concepts

Let's quickly revisit the key concepts covered in this book:

1. Understanding Energy and Mindset: The foundation of how energy and mindset shape our lives.

2. The Power of Affirmations: Crafting and using affirmations to rewire your brain.

3. Visualization Techniques: Using mental imagery to achieve your goals.

4. Breathwork Practices: Harnessing the power of breath to calm and energize.

5. Meditation for Mindset: Cultivating mindfulness and inner peace through meditation.

6. Evidence Lists: Recording daily achievements to build confidence.

7. Creating an Energy Field: Techniques to protect and enhance your personal energy.

8. Connecting to Your Inner, Divine Light: Finding and nurturing your true self.

9. Intention Setting: The importance of setting daily intentions.

10. Segmenting Your Day: Using strategic pauses to enhance focus and productivity.

11. Creating Your Personal Chart: Visualizing and tracking your progress.

12. Real-Life Applications: Success stories to inspire your journey.

Encouragement to Continue the Journey

Your journey towards a more positive and empowered life is just beginning. Continue to practice, explore, and grow. Surround yourself with supportive people and communities. Share your journey and inspire others. Remember, every day is an opportunity to start fresh and make progress.

APPENDIX

RESOURCES FOR FURTHER LEARNING AND SUPPORT

Here are some essential tools to support you on your journey. Utilize the templates and worksheets provided to track your progress and stay consistent with your practices.

Templates and Worksheets

<u>Daily Affirmation Practice</u>

Instructions: Write down a few affirmations that resonate with you and repeat them daily. Track your practice by noting the affirmations you use each day.

Example Affirmations:

1. "I am confident and capable."

2. "I trust my intuition and decisions."

3. "I am a magnet for positive energy."

<u>Visualization Practice</u>

Instructions: Spend a few minutes each day visualizing your goals and desired outcomes. Describe the scene, focus on key elements, and embrace the feelings associated with achieving your goals.

Guiding Questions:

1. What does success look like for you?

2. What are the key elements you need to focus on?

3. How do you feel when you achieve your goals?

Breathwork Practice

Instructions: Practice different breathing techniques daily to improve your well-being. Note the techniques you use and their effects.

Example Techniques:

1. 4-4-4 Energizing Breath: Inhale for 4 seconds, hold for 4 seconds, exhale for 4 seconds.

2. 3-3-3 Relaxation Breath: Inhale for 3 seconds, hold for 3 seconds, exhale for 3 seconds.

Meditation Practice

Instructions: Dedicate time each day to meditate and track your sessions. Reflect on your experience and any insights gained.

Guiding Questions:

1. How did you feel before and after meditation?

2. What thoughts or distractions came up during the session?

3. How can you improve your practice?

Evidence List Practice

Instructions: Keep a daily list of achievements and positive experiences to reinforce your progress and boost positivity.

Guiding Questions:

1. What did you accomplish today?

2. What positive experiences did you have?

3. How did these experiences make you feel?

Energy Field Visualization Practice

Instructions: Visualize a protective energy field around you each day. Note your observations and feelings during the visualization.

Guiding Questions:

1. What color and quality is your protective light?

2. How does it feel to expand this light around you?

3. What changes do you notice in your energy and mood?

Intention Setting Practice

Instructions: Set clear intentions for each day to stay focused and aligned with your goals. Reflect on your intentions and their impact.

Guiding Questions:

1. What are your main intentions for today?

2. How do these intentions align with your overall goals?

3. How do you feel after setting and acting on these intentions?

Day Segmenting Practice

Instructions: Plan your day with intentional pauses and transitions to maintain energy and productivity. Reflect on your segmenting practice.

Guiding Questions:

1. What are the key segments of your day?

2. How can you create intentional pauses to reset and refocus?

3. How do you feel after implementing these pauses?

Personal Practice Routine

Instructions: Combine various practices from the book to create a personalized daily routine. Reflect on the effectiveness and adjust as needed.

Guiding Questions:

1. What practices resonate most with you?

2. How can you integrate these practices into your daily routine?

3. What adjustments can you make to improve your routine?

Journaling Prompts

Instructions: Use these prompts to deepen your self-reflection and track your progress in various practices.

Affirmation Journal:

1. What qualities do you admire in yourself?

2. What areas do you want to improve?

3. Create an affirmation for each quality and area of improvement.

Mindfulness Journal:

1. How did you feel before and after meditation?

2. What thoughts or distractions came up during the session?

3. How can you improve your practice?

Evidence List Journal:

1. What are three things you are grateful for today?

2. Who made a positive impact on your life today?

3. What is something you appreciate about yourself?

Goal Setting Worksheet

Instructions: Set and track your short-term and long-term goals to maintain focus and direction.

1. Short-term goals (next 3 months)

Goal _____

Goal _____

Goal _____

2. Long-term goals (next 1-2 years)

Goal _____

Goal _____

Goal _____

3. Action steps to achieve these goals

Step 1: _____

Step 2: _____

Step 3: _____

CHAKRAS

UNDERSTANDING THE CHAKRAS

Introduction: Chakras are centers of energy located along the spine, each corresponding to different physical, emotional, and spiritual aspects of our being. There are seven main chakras, each with its own unique characteristics and functions. Understanding and balancing these chakras can help promote overall well-being and harmony.

1. Root Chakra (Muladhara)

- **Location:** Base of the spine

- **Color:** Red

- **Element:** Earth

- **Associated with:** Survival, security, stability

- **Signs of imbalance:** Anxiety, fear, financial instability, feeling ungrounded

- **Affirmations:** "I am safe and secure. I am grounded and stable."

2. Sacral Chakra (Svadhisthana)

- **Location:** Lower abdomen, about two inches below the navel
- **Color:** Orange
- **Element:** Water
- **Associated with:** Creativity, sexuality, pleasure, emotions
- **Signs of imbalance:** Emotional instability, lack of creativity, sexual dysfunction
- **Affirmations:** "I am creative and joyful. I embrace my sexuality."

3. Solar Plexus Chakra (Manipura)

- **Location:** Upper abdomen, near the diaphragm
- **Color:** Yellow
- **Element:** Fire
- **Associated with:** Personal power, confidence, self-esteem, willpower
- **Signs of imbalance:** Low self-esteem, lack of control, anger issues
- **Affirmations:** "I am confident and powerful. I am in control of my life."

4. Heart Chakra (Anahata)

- **Location:** Center of the chest
- **Color:** Green
- **Element:** Air
- **Associated with:** Love, compassion, forgiveness, relationships

- **Signs of imbalance:** Loneliness, jealousy, inability to forgive

- **Affirmations:** "I am open to giving and receiving love. I forgive myself and others."

5. Throat Chakra (Vishuddha)

- **Location:** Throat

- **Color:** Blue

- **Element:** Ether

- **Associated with:** Communication, expression, truth, creativity

- **Signs of imbalance:** Difficulty expressing oneself, fear of speaking, dishonesty

- **Affirmations:** "I speak my truth clearly and confidently. My voice matters."

6. Third Eye Chakra (Ajna)

- **Location:** Forehead, between the eyebrows

- **Color:** Indigo

- **Element:** Light

- **Associated with:** Intuition, wisdom, insight, imagination

- **Signs of imbalance:** Lack of intuition, confusion, difficulty focusing

- **Affirmations:** "I trust my intuition. I see things clearly."

7. Crown Chakra (Sahasrara)

- **Location:** Top of the head

- **Color:** Violet or white

- **Element:** Cosmic energy

- **Associated with:** Spirituality, enlightenment, connection to the divine

- **Signs of imbalance:** Spiritual disconnection, lack of purpose, feeling disconnected

- **Affirmations:** "I am connected to the divine. I am one with the universe."

Balancing the Chakras Balancing the chakras involves practices such as meditation, visualization, affirmations, breathwork, and energy healing. Here are a few tips to help balance each chakra:

- **Root Chakra:** Grounding exercises like walking barefoot on the earth, focusing on stability and security in your life.

- **Sacral Chakra:** Engaging in creative activities, allowing yourself to feel and express emotions freely.

- **Solar Plexus Chakra:** Practicing self-discipline, setting personal boundaries, and engaging in activities that boost confidence.

- **Heart Chakra:** Practicing compassion and forgiveness, connecting with loved ones, and engaging in heart-centered activities.

- **Throat Chakra:** Practicing clear and honest communication, singing, and using your voice.

- **Third Eye Chakra:** Meditating on the third eye, practicing visualization exercises, and listening to your intuition.

- **Crown Chakra:** Practicing mindfulness, connecting with your spiritual beliefs, and engaging in activities that promote spiritual growth.

BALANCING THE CHAKRAS

Balancing the chakras involves practices such as meditation, visualization, affirmations, breathwork, and energy healing. Here are a few tips to help balance each chakra:

- **Root Chakra:** Grounding exercises like walking barefoot on the earth, focusing on stability and security in your life.

- **Sacral Chakra:** Engaging in creative activities, allowing yourself to feel and express emotions freely.

- **Solar Plexus Chakra:** Practicing self-discipline, setting personal boundaries, and engaging in activities that boost confidence.

- **Heart Chakra:** Practicing compassion and forgiveness, connecting with loved ones, and engaging in heart-centered activities.

- **Throat Chakra:** Practicing clear and honest communication, singing, and using your voice.

- **Third Eye Chakra:** Meditating on the third eye, practicing visualization exercises, and listening to your intuition.

- **Crown Chakra:** Practicing mindfulness, connecting with your spiritual beliefs, and engaging in activities that promote spiritual growth.

AFFIRMATIONS

AFFIRMATIONS FOR RELATIONSHIP ISSUES (SPOUSE/SIGNIFICANT OTHER)

1. I am worthy of love and respect from my partner.

2. Our relationship is built on mutual love, trust, and respect.

3. We communicate openly and honestly with each other.

4. I am grateful for the love and support of my partner.

5. We resolve conflicts with compassion and understanding.

6. My partner and I grow stronger together each day.

7. I choose to see the good in my partner and our relationship.

8. Our love deepens with each passing moment.

9. We support each other's dreams and aspirations.

10. I am patient, kind, and loving in my relationship.

11. I trust my partner completely.

12. We share a deep emotional connection.

13. I am committed to nurturing our relationship.

14. We enjoy spending quality time together.

15. I appreciate my partner for who they are.
16. Our relationship is a source of joy and happiness.
17. We grow and evolve together.
18. I respect my partner's individuality.
19. We create beautiful memories together.
20. Our love is strong and enduring.

AFFIRMATIONS FOR CAREER AND JOB ISSUES

1. I am confident and capable in my job.

2. I attract opportunities that align with my skills and passions.

3. I am valued and appreciated at my workplace.

4. I am continuously growing and developing in my career.

5. My work brings me joy and fulfillment.

6. I handle challenges at work with grace and ease.

7. I am open to new opportunities and possibilities in my career.

8. I create a positive and productive work environment.

9. I am recognized for my contributions at work.

10. I am successful in all my professional endeavors.

11. I am a leader and inspire others.

12. My work is meaningful and impactful.

13. I am motivated and enthusiastic about my job.

14. I am organized and manage my time effectively.

15. I am creative and innovative in my work.

16. I am proactive and take initiative.

17. I am adaptable and embrace change.

18. I am a team player and collaborate well with others.

19. I am confident in my abilities and skills.

20. I achieve my career goals with ease.

AFFIRMATIONS FOR PARENTING AND CHILD ISSUES

1. I am a loving and patient parent.

2. My children feel safe and loved.

3. I am a positive role model for my children.

4. I communicate effectively with my children.

5. I am confident in my parenting abilities.

6. My children are happy, healthy, and thriving.

7. I support and encourage my children's dreams.

8. I handle parenting challenges with patience and understanding.

9. I am present and engaged with my children.

10. Our home is filled with love and laughter.

11. I nurture my children's individuality.

12. I create a positive and supportive environment for my children.

13. I am proud of my children's accomplishments.

14. I teach my children to be kind and compassionate.

15. I listen to my children with an open heart.

16. I guide my children with wisdom and love.

17. I am grateful for the bond I share with my children.

18. I am patient and understanding with my children's growth.

19. I celebrate my children's uniqueness.

20. I am a source of love and support for my children.

AFFIRMATIONS FOR FINANCIAL ISSUES

1. I am financially secure and abundant.

2. Money flows to me easily and effortlessly.

3. I am open to receiving financial abundance.

4. I make wise financial decisions.

5. I am grateful for the money I have.

6. I attract opportunities for financial growth.

7. I manage my finances with confidence and ease.

8. I am deserving of wealth and prosperity.

9. I am in control of my financial future.

10. I attract abundance in all areas of my life.

11. I am financially free and independent.

12. I am a good steward of my finances.

13. I create wealth and abundance in my life.

14. I am open to new streams of income.

15. I am responsible and disciplined with my money.

16. I am prosperous and financially successful.

17. I attract financial blessings and opportunities.

18. I am grateful for the financial resources I have.

19. I am wise and prudent in my financial decisions.

20. I am abundant and prosperous in all areas of my life.

AFFIRMATIONS FOR LOVE AND RELATIONSHIPS

1. I am deserving of love and happiness.
2. I attract loving and supportive relationships.
3. My heart is open to giving and receiving love.
4. I am surrounded by people who love and support me.
5. I am grateful for the love in my life.
6. I radiate love and attract it in return.
7. I am confident and secure in my relationships.
8. Love flows to me effortlessly.
9. I am worthy of a loving and fulfilling relationship.
10. I am love, and I am loved.
11. I attract positive and loving relationships.
12. I am open to deep and meaningful connections.
13. I am grateful for the loving relationships in my life.
14. I nurture my relationships with love and care.

15. I am a magnet for love and affection.

16. I attract people who respect and value me.

17. I am open to receiving unconditional love.

18. I give and receive love freely and joyfully.

19. I am surrounded by love and positivity.

20. I am worthy of all the love and happiness life has to offer.

AFFIRMATIONS FOR WEIGHT ISSUES

1. I love and accept my body as it is.

2. I am committed to achieving my weight goals.

3. I am healthy, strong, and vibrant.

4. I make choices that nourish my body and mind.

5. I am grateful for my healthy body.

6. I listen to my body's needs and honor them.

7. I am deserving of a healthy and fit body.

8. I am in control of my health and wellness.

9. I am becoming healthier and stronger each day.

10. My body is a temple, and I treat it with care.

11. I am patient and kind to myself on my weight journey.

12. I am proud of the progress I make towards my weight goals.

13. I am dedicated to maintaining a healthy lifestyle.

14. I choose foods that are nourishing and beneficial to my body.

15. I enjoy moving my body and staying active.

16. I am in tune with my body's needs and signals.

17. I am confident in my ability to reach my weight goals.

18. I celebrate every step I take towards a healthier me.

19. I love my body and treat it with respect.

20. I am grateful for my body's ability to heal and transform.

AFFIRMATIONS FOR HEALTH ISSUES

1. I am healthy, whole, and complete.

2. Every cell in my body vibrates with energy and health.

3. I am grateful for my body's strength and resilience.

4. I listen to my body and give it what it needs to thrive.

5. I am committed to my health and well-being.

6. I am in perfect health.

7. My body is a healing vessel.

8. I am strong, healthy, and vibrant.

9. I am constantly improving my health and vitality.

10. My body knows how to heal itself.

11. I am grateful for my body's ability to heal and recover.

12. I am in tune with my body's needs and signals.

13. I take care of my body by making healthy choices.

14. I am a powerful creator of my own health.

15. I am surrounded by healing energy.

16. I am committed to living a healthy and active lifestyle.

17. I am grateful for my healthy mind and body.

18. I am vibrant, healthy, and strong.

19. My body is a temple of health and well-being.

20. I am grateful for the gift of health and vitality.

AFFIRMATIONS FOR ALIGNING WITH YOUR HIGHEST SELF

1. I am in tune with my highest self.

2. I trust my intuition and inner guidance.

3. I am aligned with my purpose and passion.

4. I am connected to the infinite wisdom within me.

5. I am a powerful creator of my reality.

6. I am living a life of purpose and fulfillment.

7. I trust the journey of my life.

8. I am open to the infinite possibilities of the universe.

9. I am in harmony with the flow of life.

10. I am my highest, most authentic self.

11. I am a divine being of light and love.

12. I am connected to my inner wisdom and guidance.

13. I trust the path that is unfolding before me.

14. I am in alignment with my highest purpose.

15. I am a vessel of divine love and light.

16. I am connected to the universe and all its wisdom.

17. I am open to receiving guidance from my higher self.

18. I am living in harmony with my true self.

19. I am a co-creator with the universe.

20. I am aligned with my soul's purpose and mission.

AFFIRMATIONS FOR GENERAL WELL-BEING AND POSITIVITY

1. I am filled with positive energy and vitality.

2. I attract positivity and good vibes into my life.

3. I am grateful for the blessings in my life.

4. I am surrounded by love and abundance.

5. I choose to focus on the good in every situation.

6. I am a beacon of positivity and light.

7. I am resilient and capable of overcoming challenges.

8. I am at peace with myself and the world around me.

9. I radiate joy, love, and positivity.

10. I am grateful for each new day and the opportunities it brings.

11. I am a magnet for positive experiences.

12. I am a source of light and inspiration to others.

13. I am optimistic and confident about my future.

14. I am surrounded by positive and supportive people.

15. I choose to see the good in every person and situation.

16. I am grateful for the abundance in my life.

17. I am a positive influence on the world around me.

18. I am filled with joy and happiness.

19. I attract positive energy and experiences into my life.

20. I am living a life filled with positivity and gratitude.

VISUALIZATIONS

VISUALIZATION FOR RELATIONSHIP ISSUES (SPOUSE/SIGNIFICANT OTHER)

1. Visualization Exercise: Healing Relationship Conflicts

Find a quiet space and sit comfortably. Close your eyes and take a few deep breaths. Visualize you and your partner in a peaceful setting. Imagine having a calm, loving conversation where both of you are expressing your feelings openly and listening to each other with empathy. See the conflict resolving and feel the love and understanding between you growing stronger. Picture yourselves embracing and feeling a deep connection. Hold this image for a few minutes and then slowly bring your awareness back to the present.

2. Visualization Exercise: Strengthening the Bond

Sit in a comfortable position and close your eyes. Take deep breaths to relax. Visualize you and your partner in a beautiful location, such as a beach or a garden. See yourselves enjoying each other's company, laughing, and sharing happy moments. Feel the love and warmth between you. Imagine this bond growing stronger every day. Hold this image for a few minutes and then gently bring your awareness back to the present.

3. Visualization Exercise: Future Happiness

Find a quiet place and sit comfortably. Close your eyes and take deep breaths to relax. Visualize your future with your partner. See yourselves achieving your dreams together, supporting each other, and celebrating your successes. Picture the happiness and fulfillment you both feel. Imagine living a life full of love and joy together. Hold this vision for a few minutes before slowly returning to the present moment.

VISUALIZATION FOR CAREER AND JOB ISSUES

1. Visualization Exercise: Achieving Career Success

Sit in a comfortable position and close your eyes. Take a few deep breaths to relax. Visualize yourself in your ideal job or career situation. See yourself performing your tasks with confidence and skill. Picture your colleagues and superiors appreciating and acknowledging your work. Imagine achieving your career goals and feeling fulfilled and successful. Feel the joy and satisfaction of doing what you love. Hold this vision for a few minutes, then gradually return to the present moment.

2. Visualization Exercise: Overcoming Challenges

Find a quiet space and sit comfortably. Close your eyes and take deep breaths to relax. Visualize a challenge you are facing at work. See yourself handling it with confidence and ease. Imagine finding the perfect solution and implementing it successfully. Picture the positive outcome and the recognition you receive. Feel the relief and pride in overcoming this challenge. Hold this image for a few minutes, then slowly bring your awareness back to the present.

3. Visualization Exercise: Creating a Positive Work Environment

Sit in a comfortable position and close your eyes. Take deep breaths to relax. Visualize your workplace filled with positivity and harmony. See your colleagues working together cooperatively and respectfully. Imagine yourself feeling happy and motivated at work. Picture the environment as supportive and inspiring. Feel the positive energy and satisfaction of working in such a place. Hold this vision for a few minutes before gradually returning to the present moment.

VISUALIZATION FOR PARENTING AND CHILD ISSUES

1. Visualization Exercise: Positive Parenting

Find a quiet place and sit comfortably. Close your eyes and take deep breaths to relax. Visualize a day with your children where everything goes smoothly. See yourself interacting with your children with patience, love, and understanding. Imagine them responding positively to your guidance and support. Picture a harmonious and joyful environment at home. Feel the love and connection between you and your children. Hold this vision for a few minutes before slowly bringing your awareness back to the present.

2. Visualization Exercise: Encouraging Growth

Sit in a comfortable position and close your eyes. Take deep breaths to relax. Visualize your children achieving their goals and dreams. See them growing, learning, and becoming confident individuals. Imagine yourself supporting and encouraging them every step of the way. Picture the pride and happiness you both feel. Hold this vision for a few minutes, then gently bring your awareness back to the present moment.

3. Visualization Exercise: Family Bonding

Find a quiet space and sit comfortably. Close your eyes and take deep breaths to relax. Visualize a special family activity, such as a picnic or game night. See everyone enjoying themselves, laughing, and bonding. Imagine the love and connection growing stronger within your family. Picture the joy and togetherness you all feel. Hold this vision for a few minutes before slowly returning to the present moment.

VISUALIZATION FOR FINANCIAL ISSUES

1. Visualization Exercise: Financial Abundance

Sit in a comfortable position and close your eyes. Take a few deep breaths to relax. Visualize yourself surrounded by financial abundance. See money flowing to you easily and effortlessly. Picture yourself feeling secure and confident about your finances. Imagine using your money to achieve your goals and live a fulfilling life. Feel the gratitude and satisfaction of having financial abundance. Hold this vision for a few minutes, then gradually return to the present moment.

2. Visualization Exercise: Wise Financial Decisions

Find a quiet space and sit comfortably. Close your eyes and take deep breaths to relax. Visualize a financial decision you need to make. See yourself gathering all the necessary information and making a wise, informed choice. Imagine the positive outcome of this decision and the impact it has on your financial situation. Feel the confidence and peace of mind that comes with making wise financial decisions. Hold this image for a few minutes, then slowly bring your awareness back to the present.

3. Visualization Exercise: Financial Freedom

Sit in a comfortable position and close your eyes. Take deep breaths to relax. Visualize yourself living a life of financial freedom. See yourself free from financial worries and able to do what you love. Picture the activities and experiences you enjoy with your financial freedom. Feel the joy and liberation of being financially independent. Hold this vision for a few minutes before gradually returning to the present moment.

VISUALIZATION FOR LOVE AND RELATIONSHIPS

1. Visualization Exercise: Attracting Love

Sit in a comfortable position and close your eyes. Take a few deep breaths to relax. Visualize yourself surrounded by love. See yourself attracting a loving and supportive relationship. Picture the qualities you desire in a partner and feel the joy of having this relationship in your life. Imagine sharing happy moments and building a deep connection with your partner. Hold this vision for a few minutes, then gradually return to the present moment.

2. Visualization Exercise: Deepening Love

Find a quiet space and sit comfortably. Close your eyes and take deep breaths to relax. Visualize your current relationship deepening and growing stronger. See yourself and your partner sharing love, respect, and understanding. Imagine the bond between you becoming deeper and more meaningful. Picture the joy and fulfillment of a loving relationship. Hold this image for a few minutes before slowly bringing your awareness back to the present.

3. Visualization Exercise: Self-Love

Sit in a comfortable position and close your eyes. Take deep breaths to relax. Visualize yourself surrounded by love and light. See yourself loving and accepting yourself fully. Imagine treating yourself with kindness and compassion. Picture the positive impact of self-love on your life and relationships. Feel the joy and confidence of loving yourself unconditionally. Hold this vision for a few minutes before gradually returning to the present moment.

VISUALIZATION FOR WEIGHT ISSUES

1. Visualization Exercise: Healthy Eating

Sit in a comfortable position and close your eyes. Take a few deep breaths to relax. Visualize yourself making healthy food choices. See yourself enjoying nutritious meals that nourish your body. Picture the positive effects of healthy eating on your body and mind. Imagine feeling satisfied and energized by the food you eat. Hold this vision for a few minutes, then gradually return to the present moment.

2. Visualization Exercise: Active Lifestyle

Find a quiet space and sit comfortably. Close your eyes and take deep breaths to relax. Visualize yourself engaging in physical activities you enjoy. See yourself moving your body and feeling strong and vibrant. Imagine the positive effects of an active lifestyle on your health and well-being. Picture yourself feeling energized and happy from being active. Hold this image for a few minutes before slowly bringing your awareness back to the present.

3. Visualization Exercise: Reaching Your Ideal Weight

VISUALIZATION FOR WEIGHT ISSUES

Sit in a comfortable position and close your eyes. Take deep breaths to relax. Visualize yourself at your ideal weight. See yourself feeling confident and healthy. Picture the activities and experiences you enjoy at this weight. Imagine the positive impact on your life and self-esteem. Feel the joy and satisfaction of reaching your ideal weight. Hold this vision for a few minutes before gradually returning to the present moment.

VISUALIZATION FOR HEALTH ISSUES

1. Visualization Exercise: Healing and Recovery

Sit in a comfortable position and close your eyes. Take a few deep breaths to relax. Visualize yourself surrounded by healing light. See this light entering your body and healing any areas of discomfort or illness. Picture yourself feeling healthy, strong, and vibrant. Imagine your body recovering and becoming whole. Hold this vision for a few minutes, then gradually return to the present moment.

2. Visualization Exercise: Maintaining Good Health

Find a quiet space and sit comfortably. Close your eyes and take deep breaths to relax. Visualize yourself engaging in activities that promote good health, such as exercise, healthy eating, and relaxation. See yourself enjoying these activities and feeling the positive effects on your body and mind. Imagine yourself in perfect health, vibrant and strong. Hold this vision for a few minutes before gradually returning to the present moment.

3. Visualization Exercise: Positive Health Outcomes

116 VISUALIZATION FOR HEALTH ISSUES

Sit in a comfortable position and close your eyes. Take deep breaths to relax. Visualize yourself receiving positive health news. See yourself at a doctor's appointment, and hear the doctor telling you that you are in excellent health. Imagine the relief and happiness you feel. Picture yourself celebrating this good news with loved ones. Feel the gratitude and joy of being in great health. Hold this vision for a few minutes before gradually returning to the present moment.

VISUALIZATION FOR ALIGNING WITH YOUR HIGHEST SELF

1. Visualization Exercise: Connecting with Your Higher Self

Sit in a comfortable position and close your eyes. Take a few deep breaths to relax. Visualize yourself in a peaceful and quiet place. See yourself connecting with your higher self, the wise and loving part of you. Imagine receiving guidance and wisdom from your higher self. Picture yourself feeling aligned and in tune with your true purpose. Hold this vision for a few minutes, then gradually return to the present moment.

2. Visualization Exercise: Manifesting Your Dreams

Find a quiet space and sit comfortably. Close your eyes and take deep breaths to relax. Visualize your biggest dreams and goals. See yourself achieving them and living the life you desire. Imagine the steps you take to manifest these dreams and the support you receive along the way. Picture the joy and fulfillment of living your dreams. Hold this vision for a few minutes before slowly bringing your awareness back to the present.

3. Visualization Exercise: Living in Alignment

Sit in a comfortable position and close your eyes. Take deep breaths to relax. Visualize yourself living a life that is fully aligned with your highest self. See yourself making choices that honor your values and beliefs. Imagine feeling peaceful, content, and fulfilled. Picture yourself surrounded by positive energy and living your purpose. Hold this vision for a few minutes before gradually returning to the present moment.

VISUALIZATION FOR GENERAL WELL-BEING AND POSITIVITY

1. Visualization Exercise: Daily Positivity

Sit in a comfortable position and close your eyes. Take a few deep breaths to relax. Visualize yourself starting your day with a positive mindset. See yourself going through your day with a smile, handling challenges with ease, and spreading positivity to those around you. Imagine the impact of your positive energy on your day. Hold this vision for a few minutes, then gradually return to the present moment.

2. Visualization Exercise: Inner Peace

Find a quiet space and sit comfortably. Close your eyes and take deep breaths to relax. Visualize yourself in a peaceful setting, such as a beach or a garden. See yourself feeling calm and centered. Imagine the feeling of inner peace and tranquility spreading throughout your body. Picture yourself carrying this sense of peace with you throughout your day. Hold this vision for a few minutes before slowly bringing your awareness back to the present.

3. Visualization Exercise: Gratitude Practice

Sit in a comfortable position and close your eyes. Take deep breaths to relax. Visualize the things you are grateful for in your life. See yourself appreciating the small and big blessings. Imagine the feeling of gratitude filling your heart and radiating outwards. Picture the positive impact of gratitude on your well-being and happiness. Hold this vision for a few minutes before gradually returning to the present moment.

4. Visualization Exercise: Creating an Ideal Day

Sit in a comfortable position and close your eyes. Take deep breaths to relax. Visualize your ideal day from start to finish. See yourself waking up feeling refreshed and excited. Picture yourself going through your day with ease, achieving your goals, and enjoying positive interactions. Imagine the feeling of satisfaction and joy at the end of the day. Hold this vision for a few minutes before gradually returning to the present moment.

5. Visualization Exercise: Overcoming Obstacles

Find a quiet space and sit comfortably. Close your eyes and take deep breaths to relax. Visualize a challenge or obstacle you are currently facing. See yourself approaching it with confidence and determination. Imagine finding a solution and successfully overcoming the obstacle. Picture the feeling of accomplishment and relief. Hold this vision for a few minutes before slowly bringing your awareness back to the present.

6. Visualization Exercise: Achieving Balance

Sit in a comfortable position and close your eyes. Take deep breaths to relax. Visualize yourself balancing different aspects of your life, such as work, family, and personal time. See yourself managing your time and energy effectively. Imagine feeling balanced, fulfilled, and at peace. Picture the positive impact of this balance on your overall well-being. Hold this vision for a few minutes before gradually returning to the present moment.

GLOSSARY

Affirmation: A positive statement that is repeated to reinforce a desired belief or outcome. Affirmations are used to reprogram the subconscious mind.

Alignment: The state of being in harmony with one's true self, values, and purpose. Achieving alignment involves making choices that reflect one's authentic self.

Breathwork: A practice involving conscious control of breathing patterns to improve mental, emotional, and physical well-being. Breathwork can reduce stress and enhance relaxation.

Chakra: Centers of energy in the body, traditionally recognized in Eastern spiritual practices. There are seven main chakras, each associated with different aspects of physical and emotional health.

Empowerment: The process of gaining confidence and control over one's life. Empowerment involves recognizing one's abilities and taking action towards goals.

Energy Field: An invisible field of energy that surrounds and permeates the body. It is believed to reflect and influence one's physical and emotional state.

Frequency: The vibration or energy level at which a person operates. Higher frequencies are associated with positive emotions and states of being.

Gratitude: The practice of recognizing and appreciating the positive aspects of life. Gratitude can improve mental health and attract more positive experiences.

Grounding: A practice of connecting with the earth's energy to achieve balance and stability. Grounding techniques include walking barefoot on the earth or visualizing roots connecting to the ground.

Inner Light: The inherent wisdom, love, and divinity within each person. Connecting with one's inner light involves recognizing and embracing this inner source of guidance and strength.

Inner Peace: A state of mental and emotional calmness. Inner peace is achieved through practices such as meditation, mindfulness, and self-reflection.

Intention Setting: The act of defining a specific goal or desired outcome. Setting intentions helps to focus the mind and align actions with desired results.

Limiting Beliefs: Negative beliefs that restrict one's potential and success. Overcoming limiting beliefs involves recognizing and replacing them with empowering thoughts.

Manifestation: The process of bringing desired outcomes into reality through focused intention and positive energy. Manifestation involves aligning thoughts, beliefs, and actions with one's goals.

Meditation: A practice of focused attention and mindfulness to achieve a mentally clear and emotionally calm state. Meditation can reduce stress and enhance overall well-being.

Mindfulness: The practice of being present and fully engaged in the current moment. Mindfulness enhances awareness and reduces stress.

Mindset: The set of beliefs and attitudes that shape one's perception and approach to life. A positive mindset can enhance resilience and success.

Mirror Work: A practice of looking at oneself in the mirror while repeating positive affirmations. Mirror work helps to build self-love and confidence.

Positive Thinking: Focusing on positive thoughts and attitudes. Positive thinking can improve mental health and attract positive experiences.

Reiki: A Japanese healing technique that involves channeling energy to promote relaxation and healing. Reiki practitioners use their hands to transfer energy to the recipient.

Resilience: The ability to recover quickly from difficulties and adapt to challenges. Building resilience involves cultivating a positive mindset and coping strategies.

Self-Care: The practice of taking actions to improve one's physical, emotional, and mental health. Self-care includes activities that promote relaxation and well-being.

Self-Love: The practice of accepting and valuing oneself. Self-love involves treating oneself with kindness and compassion.

Sound Healing: The use of sound frequencies, such as music, singing bowls, or tuning forks, to promote healing and relaxation. Sound healing can reduce stress and enhance mental clarity.

Subconscious Mind: The part of the mind that operates below the level of conscious awareness. The subconscious mind influences beliefs, behaviors, and emotions.

Visualization: The practice of creating mental images of desired outcomes. Visualization helps to align the subconscious mind with goals and increase motivation.

Well-Being: A state of being comfortable, healthy, and happy. Well-being encompasses physical, emotional, and mental health.

ACKNOWLEDGMENTS

I want to express my heartfelt gratitude to all of my clients. Your journeys have taught me so much, and I continue to grow and learn from each of you every day.

To my three boys, Henry, Charlie, and Teddy, thank you for just being you and for being open to expanding your knowledge of energy and mindset every day. A special thank you to Henry for helping me with technology and the design of this book cover! To Charlie, thank you for meeting with me and practicing these tools. And to Teddy, thank you for helping us all 'change our radio stations' when needed.

To my husband, Jared, your unwavering support means the world to me.

To my dear friend Anna Brooke, who saw this spark in me, encouraged me to follow this path, and recognized my gifts—I am forever grateful.

I hope through my teachings and this book that I help others find their gifts and passion too. Thank you all for being a part of this journey.

ABOUT THE AUTHOR

With over two decades of experience as a pioneering leader in facilitating profound transformation for individuals and corporate teams, Katherine MacLane is recognized as a standout authority in the realms of energy coaching, healing, and mindset transformation. Through scientifically-backed methods, she facilitates shifts in vibrations and frequencies, unlocking the most authentic and empowered versions of her clients both in-person and virtually. Katherine's journey is propelled by an unwavering dedication to guiding others towards inner fulfillment and profound self-discovery.

Throughout her career, Katherine has been featured in esteemed publications such as the Wall Street Journal, CBS Sunday Morning, Forbes, and numerous other national and international media outlets. She holds education from Southern Methodist University and the Kellogg School of Management. Katherine is also certified in Reiki, Energy Healing, Mindset and Life Coaching, Chakras, Crystals, and Sound Frequency Healing.